JIGSAW JOURNEY

THE 50 STATES

Ruth Strother

Silver Dolphin

Silver Dolphin Books
An imprint of Printers Row Publishing Group
A division of Readerlink Distribution Services, LLC
9717 Pacific Heights Blvd, San Diego, CA 92121
www.silverdolphinbooks.com

Printers Row Publishing Group is a division of Readerlink Distribution Services, LLC.
Silver Dolphin Books is a registered trademark of Readerlink Distribution Services, LLC.
The name of the Smithsonian Institution and the sunburst logo are registered trademarks of the Smithsonian Institution. For more information, please visit www.si.edu.
All notations of errors or omissions should be addressed to Silver Dolphin Books, Editorial Department, at the above address.

A component of 978-1-6672-1329-3. Not for individual sale.
Manufactured, printed, and assembled in Shaoguan, China.
First printing, February 2026. SL/02/26
30 29 28 27 26 1 2 3 4 5

Written by Ruth Strother
Puzzle and poster art by Sara Lynn Cramb
Book and package design by Haydee Yanez

For Smithsonian Enterprises:
Paige Towler, Editorial Lead, Licensed Publishing
Jill Corcoran, Senior Director, Licensed Publishing
Brigid Ferraro, Vice President of New Business and Licensing
Carol LeBlanc, President

WELCOME

to

The United States of America is one nation made up of 50 individual states, and the city-state of Washington, D.C.. Each state is as special as the people that live in our amazing country. From mile-high mountains to scorching-hot deserts, from forests with trees older than our country to white sand beaches, some of the most beautiful scenery in the world is found right here. America has an incredible history and is home to some pretty impressive people too. This book is full of great facts about these 50 states, but let's start with some quick facts about their home: the United States of America.

National Capital: Washington, D.C.

National Population: Over 340 million

Area of Land: Over 3.5 million square miles

Independence Day: July 4, 1776

United States Bird: American Bald Eagle

United States Flower: Rose

Alabama (AL)

Nicknames
The Heart of Dixie; The Yellowhammer State; The Cotton State

State Capital: Montgomery

Date of Statehood: Alabama became the 22nd state on December 14, 1819

State Bird: Yellowhammer, also known as the northern flicker

State Mammal: Black bear

State Flower: Camellia

FAMOUS PEOPLE FROM ALABAMA:

★ **Rosa Parks**, *a civil rights activist, was born in Tuskegee, Alabama.*

★ *Pulitzer Prize–winning author* **Harper Lee** *was born in Monroeville, Alabama.*

★ *Gold medal Olympian* **Jesse Owens** *was born in Oakville, Alabama.*

★ DID YOU KNOW? ★

- The first rocket to fly humans to the Moon was made in Huntsville, Alabama.

- The World Championship Domino Tournament is held in Andalusia, Alabama. But it is against the law to play dominoes anywhere in Alabama on Sundays.

- According to legend, it's against the law to wear a fake mustache to church just to make people laugh.

Alaska (AK)

Nicknames: The Last Frontier; The Great Land; The Land of the Midnight Sun

State Capital: Juneau

Date of Statehood: Alaska became the 49th state on January 3, 1959

State Bird: Willow Ptarmigan

State Mammal: Moose

State Flower: Forget-Me-Not

- For 84 days of the year, the Sun never sets in Barrow, Alaska, which is the northernmost city in the United States.

- There is no way to drive into Juneau, Alaska's capital. You can get there only by plane or ferry.

- Nobody ever lived in igloos. They were used only as temporary or emergency shelters. People still use igloos for part-time protection, using the same building methods they used centuries ago.

FAMOUS PEOPLE FROM ALASKA:

★ **Libby Riddles** was the first woman to win the Iditarod dog sled race in 1985.

★ **Susan Butcher** won the Iditarod three years in a row.

★ **Benny Benson** was 13 years old when he designed the state flag—32 years before Alaska became a state!

Arizona (AZ)

Nickname: The Grand Canyon State

State Capital: Phoenix

Date of Statehood: Arizona became the 48th state on February 14, 1912

State Bird: Cactus Wren

State Mammal: Ringtail

State Flower: Saguaro Cactus Blossom

FAMOUS PEOPLE FROM ARIZONA:

★ **Cesar Chavez**, *labor leader.*

★ **Goyakla (a.k.a. Geronimo)**, *Apache chief.*

★ **Sandra Day O'Connor**, *the first woman appointed to the United States Supreme Court, grew up on a cattle ranch near Duncan, Arizona.*

★ DID YOU KNOW? ★

• The saguaro cactus of southern Arizona is the biggest cactus in the United States, and it can live for up to 200 years!

• The layer of rock at the bottom of the Colorado River, which cuts through Arizona's Grand Canyon, is almost two billion years old.

• The original London Bridge was built in England in 1831, taken apart in 1967, and reconstructed in Lake Havasu City, Arizona, in 1971.

Arkansas (AR)

Nickname: The Natural State

State Capital: Little Rock

Date of Statehood: Arkansas became the 25th state on June 15, 1836

State Bird: Mockingbird

State Mammal: White-Tailed Deer

State Flower: Apple Blossom

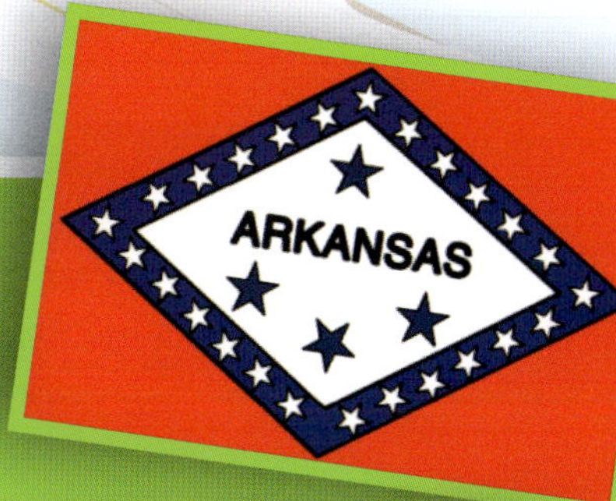

California (CA)

Nickname: The Golden State

State Capital: Sacramento

Date of Statehood: California became the 31st state on September 9, 1850

State Bird: California Valley Quail

State Mammal: Grizzly Bear

State Flower: California Poppy

FAMOUS PEOPLE FROM CALIFORNIA:

★ **Steve Jobs**, founder of the Apple computer and creator of the iPhone.

★ **Sally Ride**, astronaut and first American woman to go into space.

★ **Ellen Ochoa**, astronaut and first Latina woman to go into space.

★ **Ronald Reagan**, actor, governor, and 40th president of the United States, lived in California.

★ DID YOU KNOW? ★

• California's Death Valley is the hottest and driest place in the United States. The temperature in the summer is usually over 120°F, and it rains less than two inches a year if it rains at all.

• Magic Castle in Hollywood, California, is the headquarters for the Academy of Magical Arts. Only magicians and their guests are allowed in. And, you have to know the secret password.

• The Methuselah Tree, a Great Basin bristlecone pine, is older than the Egyptian pyramids. It grows in the White Mountains of California, but its exact whereabouts are a secret to protect it from vandals.

Colorado (CO)

Nickname: The Centennial State

State Capital: Denver

Date of Statehood: Colorado became the 38th state on August 1, 1876

State Bird: Lark Bunting

State Mammal: Rocky Mountain Bighorn Sheep

State Flower: White and Lavender Rocky Mountain Columbine

FAMOUS PEOPLE FROM COLORADO:

★ *John "Jack" Swigert*, an astronaut on the failed Apollo 13 space mission, reported, "Okay, Houston, we've had a problem here."

★ *Margaret "Molly" Brown* lived in Denver, Colorado, and is known for saving lives aboard the *Titanic* after it collided with an iceberg and sank.

★ DID YOU KNOW? ★

• The NIST-F1 Cesium Fountain Atomic Clock in Boulder, Colorado, keeps time for the entire country. It will be accurate to the second for 80 million years!

• Colorado's Florissant Fossil Beds National Monument is home to huge petrified redwood trees and the most fossilized insects in the world.

• Denver considers its Colfax Avenue to be the longest commercial street in the United States, at 26.5 miles.

Connecticut (CT)

Nickname: The Constitution State

State Capital: Hartford

Date of Statehood: Connecticut became the 5th state on January 9, 1788

State Bird: American Robin

State Mammal: Sperm Whale

State Flower: Mountain Laurel

FAMOUS PERSON FROM CONNECTICUT:

★ *P. T. Barnum, born in Bethel, Connecticut, started a circus he called The Greatest Show on Earth. It eventually became the Ringling Bros. and Barnum & Bailey Greatest Show on Earth.*

Delaware (DE)

FAMOUS PERSON FROM DELAWARE:

★ *Before he was the 46th president of the United States,* **Joe Biden** *became a senator representing Delaware when he was just 29 years old.*

Nickname: The First State

State Capital: Dover

Date of Statehood: Delaware became the first state on December 7, 1787

State Bird: Blue Hen Chicken

State Mammal: Gray Fox

State Flower: Peach Blossom

• Delaware was the first state to fly the American flag.

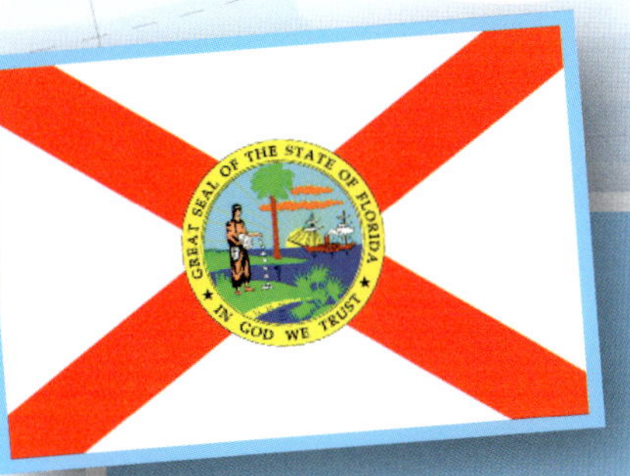

Florida (FL)

Nickname: The Sunshine State

State Capital: Tallahassee

Date of Statehood: Florida became the 27th state on March 3, 1845

State Bird: Mockingbird

State Mammal: Florida Panther

State Flower: Orange Blossom

FAMOUS PEOPLE FROM FLORIDA:

★ **Zora Neale Hurston**, African American writer, anthropologist, and folklorist, grew up in Eatonville, Florida.

★ **Norman Thagard**, born in Marianna, Florida, was the first American to jettison into outer space aboard a Russian spaceship and is considered to be the first American cosmonaut.

Georgia (GA)

Nicknames: The Peach State; The Empire State of the South

State Capital: Atlanta

Date of Statehood: Georgia became the 4th state on January 2, 1788

State Bird: Brown Thrasher

State Mammal: Right Whale

State Flower: Cherokee Rose

FAMOUS PEOPLE FROM GEORGIA:

★ *Juliette Gordon Low*, born in Savannah, Georgia, was the founder of the Girl Scouts.

★ *Jackie Robinson*, born in Cairo, Georgia, was the first African American Major League Baseball player.

★ *Martin Luther King Jr.*, civil rights leader.

★ DID YOU KNOW? ★

• The first U.S. gold rush did not take place in California; it took place in Dahlonega, Georgia in 1828.

• Coca-Cola was "born" in 1886 in Atlanta, Georgia, when pharmacist John S. Pemberton combined his specially created syrup with carbonated water.

• More peanuts are grown in Georgia than in any other state in the country.

- Mauna Kea, on the island of Hawaii, is an inactive volcano that's so big and heavy that it's sinking little by little into the ocean floor.

- The Dole pineapple plantation in Oahu has the biggest pineapple maze.

- Hawaii is the only state in the nation that is getting bigger, thanks to all of its active volcanoes.

Hawaii (HI)

Nickname: The Aloha State

State Capital: Honolulu

Date of Statehood: Hawaii became the 50th state on August 21, 1959

State Bird: Nene

State Mammal: Humpback Whale

State Flower: Pua Aloalo (Yellow Hibiscus)

FAMOUS PEOPLE FROM HAWAII:

★ *Lili'uokalani*, the first queen and the last monarch of Hawaii.

★ *Barack Obama*, first African American president of the United States, was born in Honolulu, Hawaii.

Idaho (ID)

Nickname: The Gem State

State Capital: Boise

Date of Statehood: Idaho became the 43rd state on July 3, 1890

State Bird: Mountain Bluebird

State Mammal: Appaloosa Horse

State Flower: Syringa

FAMOUS PERSON FROM IDAHO:

★ **Ernest Hemingway** won the Nobel Prize in Literature and lived in Sun Valley, Idaho, while writing *For Whom the Bell Tolls*.

★ DID YOU KNOW? ★

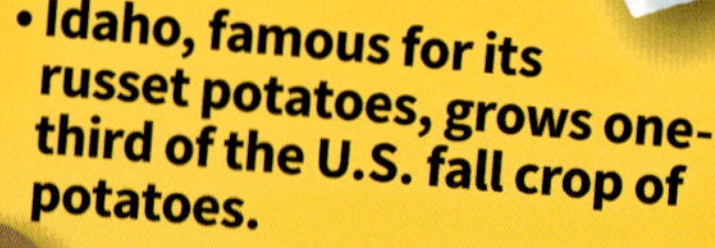

- Idaho has more rivers than any other state.

- One of the biggest diamonds found in the United States was from McCall, Idaho.

- Idaho, famous for its russet potatoes, grows one-third of the U.S. fall crop of potatoes.

Illinois (IL)

Nickname: The Prairie State

State Capital: Springfield

Date of Statehood: Illinois became the 21st state on December 3, 1818

State Bird: Northern Cardinal

State Mammal: White-Tailed Deer

State Flower: Purple Violet

★ DID YOU KNOW? ★

- The Home Insurance Building, built in Chicago in 1885, is the world's first skyscraper. It was only 10 stories high.

- The official snack food of Illinois is popcorn.

FAMOUS PEOPLE FROM ILLINOIS:

★ **Walt Disney**, born in Chicago, Illinois, was Mickey Mouse's creator and founder of Disneyland.

★ **George Ferris**, engineer and inventor of the Ferris wheel.

Indiana (IN)

Nickname: The Hoosier State

State Capital: Indianapolis

Date of Statehood: Indiana became the 19th state on December 11, 1816

State Bird: Northern Cardinal

State Flower: Peony

★ DID YOU KNOW? ★

- A city in Indiana called Santa Claus gets more than half a million letters to Santa every year around Christmas.

- Rather than being called "Indianans," residents of Indiana are traditionally called "Hoosiers."

- In Indiana, it's against the law to catch fish with dynamite or with your hands.

- The Indy 500, a 500-mile car race that is one of the most respected motorsports events in the world, takes place on Memorial Day weekend in Speedway, Indiana.

Iowa (IA)

Nickname: Hawkeye State

State Capital: Des Moines

Date of Statehood: Iowa became the 29th state on December 28, 1846

State Bird: Eastern Goldfinch

State Flower: Wild Rose

FAMOUS PEOPLE FROM IOWA:

★ **Buffalo Bill (a.k.a. William Cody)**, *Pony Express rider and showman, was born in Le Claire, Iowa.*

★ **Herbert Hoover**, *the 31st president of the United States, was born in West Branch, Iowa.*

- The first corn palace was built in Sioux City, Iowa. Covered with corn and grain, it spanned 18,000 square feet.

- Iowa is the only state in the country that is sandwiched between rivers. The Mississippi River flows along Iowa's entire eastern border, and the Missouri River, along with its tributary the Big Sioux, form the entire western border.

- Snake Alley in Burlington, Iowa, was named "unbelievably crooked" by *Ripley's Believe It or Not!*

Kansas (KS)

Nickname: The Sunflower State

State Capital: Topeka

Date of Statehood: Kansas became the 34th state on January 29, 1861

State Bird: Western Meadowlark

State Mammal: American Bison

State Flower: Wild Native Sunflower

KANSAS

FAMOUS PEOPLE FROM KANSAS:

★ Underwater archaeologist **Robert Ballard**, born in Wichita, Kansas, discovered the sunken *Titanic* and other notable ships.

★ **Amelia Earhart**, born in Atchison, Kansas, was the first woman to fly across the Pacific and Atlantic Oceans. She vanished as she was attempting the first around-the-world flight by a woman.

Kentucky (KY)

Nickname: The Bluegrass State

State Capital: Frankfort

Date of Statehood: Kentucky became the 15th state on June 1, 1792

State Bird: Northern Cardinal

State Mammal: Gray Squirrel

State Flower: Goldenrod

FAMOUS PEOPLE FROM KENTUCKY:

★ The song "Happy Birthday to You" was written in 1893 by sisters **Patty and Mildred Hill**, who were teachers in Louisville, Kentucky.

★ **Cassius Marcellus Clay Jr. (a.k.a. Muhammad Ali)**, three-time world heavyweight boxing champion, was born in Louisville, Kentucky.

★ DID YOU KNOW? ★

• The Kentucky Derby, held in Louisville, Kentucky, is the oldest horse race in the United States.

• Middlesboro, Kentucky, is the only city in the United States that was built inside a meteorite crater.

• More than 425 miles of Kentucky's Mammoth Cave have been explored so far, making it the world's longest cave system.

Louisiana (LA)

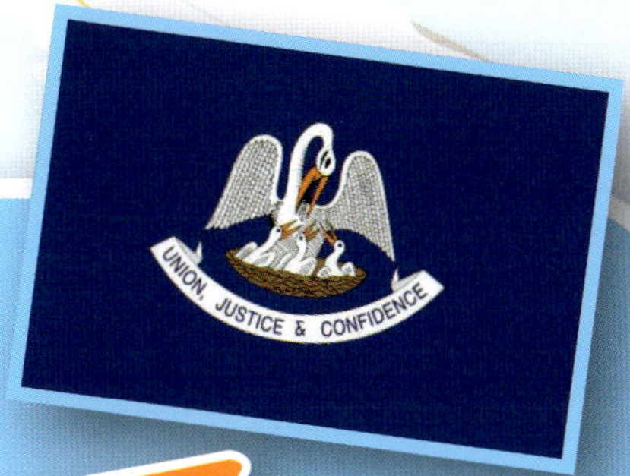

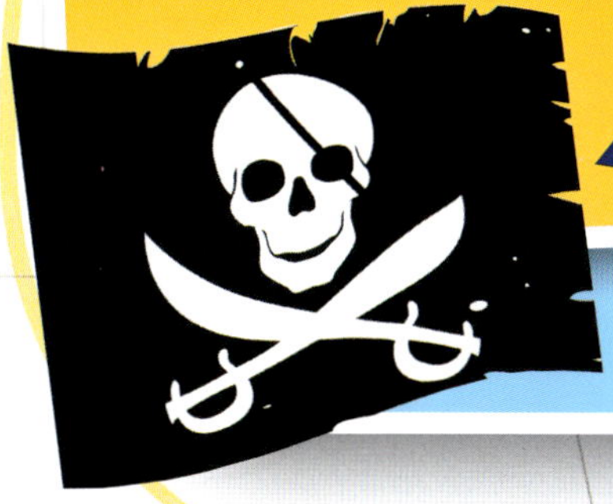

Nickname: The Pelican State

State Capital: Baton Rouge

Date of Statehood: Louisiana became the 18th state on April 30, 1812

State Bird: Brown Pelican

State Mammal: Louisiana Black Bear

State Flower: Magnolia

Maine (ME)

Nickname: The Pine Tree State

State Capital: Augusta

Date of Statehood: Maine became the 23rd state on March 15, 1820

State Bird: Black-Capped Chickadee

State Mammal: Moose

State Flower: White Pine Cone and Tassel

FAMOUS PERSON FROM MAINE:

★ *Milton Bradley*, born in Vienna, Maine, created board games and printed kindergarten materials in English for the first time in the United States.

★ DID YOU KNOW? ★

- More than 60 lighthouses shine their beacons from the craggy coast of Maine.

- The Maine lobster is a cold-water lobster with two big claws, one used for ripping prey, and the bigger one used for crushing prey.

Maryland (MD)

Nickname: The Old Line State

State Capital: Annapolis

Date of Statehood: Maryland became the 7th state on April 28, 1788

State Bird: Baltimore Oriole

State Flower: Black-Eyed Susan

★ DID YOU KNOW? ★

- In Baltimore on June 24, 1784, 13-year-old Edward Warren became the first person in the United States to be successfully launched in a balloon.

- The first umbrellas in the United States were produced in Baltimore.

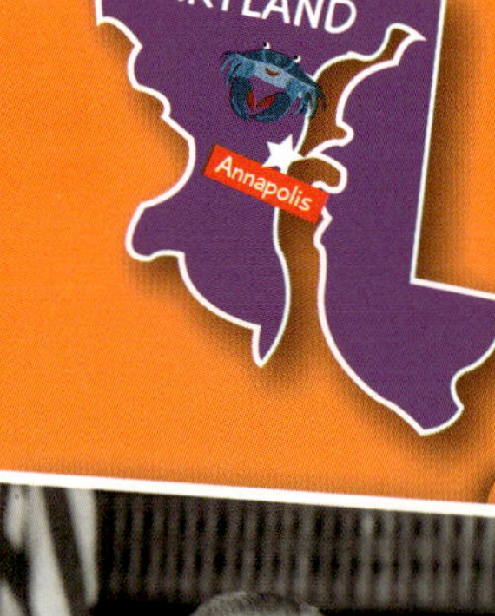

FAMOUS PERSON FROM MARYLAND:

★ *Thurgood Marshall*, born in Baltimore, Maryland, was the first African American justice of the United States Supreme Court.

Massachusetts (MA)

 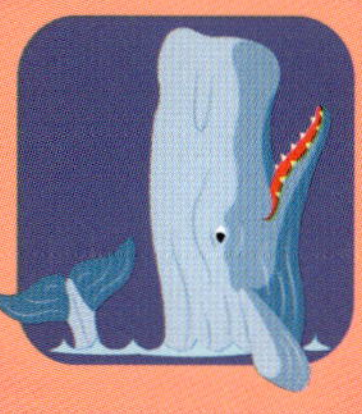 

Nickname: The Bay State

State Capital: Boston

Date of Statehood: Massachusetts became the 6th state on February 6, 1788

State Bird: Black-Capped Chickadee

State Mammal: Right Whale

State Flower: Mayflower

FAMOUS PEOPLE FROM MASSACHUSETTS:

★ *Johnny Appleseed (a.k.a. John Chapman)*, born in Leominster, Massachusetts, scattered apple seeds around the country.

★ *Denjamin Franklin,* one of the Founding Fathers and an inventor, was born in Boston, Massachusetts.

★ *John F. Kennedy*, born in Brookline, Massachusetts, became the 35th president in 1961 and was assassinated in 1963.

★ DID YOU KNOW? ★

• A gym teacher in Springfield, Massachusetts, invented the game of basketball.

• The Boston University Bridge is the only bridge in the United States where a boat can sail under a train, that is choo-chooing under a car, that is driving under an airplane.

• Over one million people a year come from all over the world to visit Pilgrim Memorial State Park in Plymouth, Massachusetts, to view Plymouth Rock.

• The pedal-powered swan boats have ferried passengers on tours of Boston's Public Garden since the 1870s.

• Alexander Graham Bell made the first telephone call from his Boston, Massachusetts, laboratory in 1876.

Michigan (MI)

Nicknames: The Great Lakes State; Wolverine State

State Capital: Lansing

Date of Statehood: Michigan became the 26th state on January 26, 1837

State Bird: American Robin

State Mammal: White-Tailed Deer

State Flower: Apple Blossom

FAMOUS PEOPLE FROM MICHIGAN:

★ **Will Keith Kellogg** invented breakfast cereal and founded the Kellogg Company and Kellogg's Corn Flakes.

★ **Henry Ford**, born in Greenfield Township, Michigan, invented the assembly line for mass production and the Model T automobile.

★ DID YOU KNOW? ★

- Grand Haven, Michigan, is known for the "singing" sand on its beach. The sand doesn't actually sing, but it does whistle and squeak.

- Detroit, Michigan, became known as the car capital of the world in 1946.

- Michigan State University has a collection of 156 mammal brains.

- Michigan borders four of the five Great Lakes, making it the world's longest freshwater coastline.

- Michigan grows up to 75 percent of the tart cherries in the United States.

Minnesota (MN)

Nicknames: The North Star State; The Land of 10,000 Lakes

State Capital: St. Paul

Date of Statehood: Minnesota became the 32nd state on May 11, 1858

State Bird: Loon

State Flower: Pink and White Lady's Slipper

FAMOUS PEOPLE FROM MINNESOTA:

★ **Laura Ingalls Wilder**, author of *Little House on the Prairie*, lived on Plum Creek near Walnut Grove, Minnesota.

★ **Charles Schulz**, born in Minneapolis, created Charlie Brown and the *Peanuts* comic strip.

★ **Judy Garland**, who played Dorothy in *The Wizard of Oz*, was born in Grand Rapids, Minnesota.

Mississippi (MS)

Nickname: The Magnolia State

State Capital: Jackson

Date of Statehood: Mississippi became the 20th state on December 10, 1817

State Bird: Mockingbird

State Mammals: White-Tailed Deer and Red Fox

State Flower: Magnolia

FAMOUS PERSON FROM MISSISSIPPI:

★ *Elvis Presley, the king of rock and roll, was born in Tupelo, Mississippi.*

★ DID YOU KNOW? ★

- The only cactus plantation in the world can be found in Edwards, Mississippi.

- Farming catfish is a big industry in Mississippi, which produces over 50 percent of the catfish in the United States.

Missouri (MO)

Nickname: The Show-Me State

State Capital: Jefferson City

Date of Statehood: Missouri became the 24th state on August 10, 1821

State Bird: Bluebird

State Mammal: Missouri Mule

State Flower: Hawthorn

★ DID YOU KNOW? ★

- The ice cream cone was invented at the St. Louis World's Fair in 1904 when an ice cream vendor ran out of cups and asked a waffle vendor to roll up waffles as a way to hold ice cream.

- The Pony Express started in St. Joseph, Missouri.

FAMOUS PERSON FROM MISSOURI:

★ *Samuel L. Clemens (a.k.a. Mark Twain), born in Florida, Missouri, wrote* The Adventures of Tom Sawyer *and* The Adventures of Huckleberry Finn, *among many other books.*

Montana (MT)

Nickname: The Treasure State

State Capital: Helena

Date of Statehood: Montana became the 41st state on November 8, 1889

State Bird: Western Meadowlark

State Mammal: Grizzly Bear

State Flower: Bitterroot

FAMOUS PEOPLE FROM MONTANA:

★ Motorcycle daredevil **Robert Craig Knievel (a.k.a. Evel Knievel)** was born in Butte, Montana.

★ **Jack Horner**, born in Shelby, Montana, discovered many dinosaur species and inspired *Jurassic Park's* Dr. Alan Grant.

★ DID YOU KNOW? ★

- Montana is called the Treasure State because of all the gold, silver, and copper buried under its mountains.

- Montana's Glacier National Park contains remnants of glaciers nearly 10,000 years old.

- Little Bighorn Battlefield in Crow Agency, Montana, is a national monument to the famous battle between the U.S. Army, led by General George Custer, and the Lakota, Cheyenne, and Arapaho Native American tribes.

Nebraska (NE)

Nickname: The Corn Husker State

State Capital: Lincoln

Date of Statehood: Nebraska became the 37th state on March 1, 1867

State Bird: Western Meadowlark

State Mammal: White-Tailed Deer

State Flower: Goldenrod

★ DID YOU KNOW? ★

- One of the biggest woolly mammoth fossils was found in Lincoln, Nebraska.

- Hebron, Nebraska, claims the world's biggest porch swing. It can seat a whole classroom of kids!

FAMOUS PERSON FROM NEBRASKA:

★ *Gerald Ford*, the 38th president of the United States, was born in Omaha, Nebraska.

Nevada (NV)

Nickname: The Silver State

State Capital: Carson City

Date of Statehood: Nevada became the 36th state on October 31, 1864

State Bird: Mountain Bluebird

State Mammal: Desert Bighorn Sheep

State Flower: Sagebrush

FAMOUS PERSON FROM NEVADA:

★ *Sarah Winnemucca*, Northern Paiute activist and author, established Nevada's first school for Native Americans.

★ DID YOU KNOW? ★

- There is enough concrete in the Hoover Dam on the Nevada-Arizona border to build a four-foot-wide sidewalk around the earth's equator.

- Nevada produces more gold than any other state in the nation.

New Hampshire (NH)

Nickname: The Granite State

State Capital: Concord

Date of Statehood: New Hampshire became the 9th state on June 21, 1788

State Bird: Purple Finch

State Mammal: White-Tailed Deer

State Flower: Purple Lilac

- The first potato planted in the United States was in 1719 at New Hampshire's Londonderry Common Field.

- The first alarm clock was invented in Concord, New Hampshire.

- Peterborough, New Hampshire, opened the first public library in the United States.

FAMOUS PEOPLE FROM NEW HAMPSHIRE:

★ **Sharon Christa McAuliffe** taught school in Concord, New Hampshire. She was one of the seven crew members killed in the space shuttle Challenger disaster in 1986.

★ **Alan Shepard**, born in Derry, New Hampshire, was the first American to travel into space.

New Jersey (NJ)

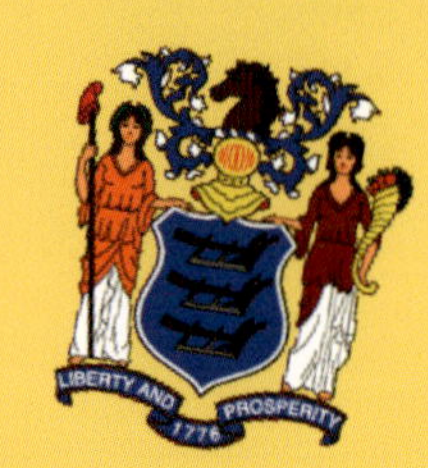

FAMOUS PEOPLE FROM NEW JERSEY:

★ *Astronaut **Edwin "Buzz" Aldrin**, born in Montclair, New Jersey, was the second person to walk on the Moon.*

★ ***Paul Robeson**, born in Princeton, New Jersey, was a professional football player, lawyer, singer, actor, and civil rights activist.*

Nickname: The Garden State

State Capital: Trenton

Date of Statehood: New Jersey became the 3rd state on December 18, 1787

State Bird: Eastern Goldfinch

State Mammal: Horse

State Flower: Violet

★ DID YOU KNOW? ★

- Thomas Edison invented the lightbulb in Menlo Park, New Jersey.

- The street names for the game Monopoly come from Atlantic City, New Jersey.

- The first baseball game was played in Hoboken, New Jersey.

New Mexico (NM)

★ DID YOU KNOW? ★

- The world's biggest hot-air balloon exhibit comes to Albuquerque, New Mexico, every October.

- The American International Rattlesnake Museum in Albuquerque, New Mexico, has the world's biggest collection of live rattlesnakes.

- Adobe (a mix of sand, straw, soil, and water) is used to build many homes in New Mexico.

Nickname: The Land of Enchantment

State Capital: Santa Fe

Date of Statehood: New Mexico became the 47th state on January 6, 1912

State Bird: Greater Roadrunner

State Mammal: Black Bear

State Flower: Yucca

FAMOUS PEOPLE FROM NEW MEXICO:

★ **William Hanna**, born in Melrose, New Mexico, was the cofounder of Hanna-Barbera and created the Flintstones and Yogi Bear.

★ **John Denver**, born in Roswell, New Mexico, was a singer, songwriter, actor, and humanitarian.

★ **Georgia O'Keeffe** painted many of her most famous works while living in New Mexico.

New York (NY)

Nickname: The Empire State

State Capital: Albany

Date of Statehood: New York became the 11th state on July 26, 1788

State Bird: Eastern Bluebird

State Mammal: Beaver

State Flower: Rose

FAMOUS PEOPLE FROM NEW YORK:

★ **Franklin Delano Roosevelt**, born in Hyde Park, New York, was the 32nd president of the United States.

★ **Donald J. Trump** was twice elected president of the United States, in 2016 and 2024.

★ **Jonas Salk**, born in New York City, invented and developed the polio vaccine.

★ DID YOU KNOW? ★

- The Oz-Stravaganza festival is held in Chittenango, New York, home of *The Wonderful Wizard of Oz* author L. Frank Baum.

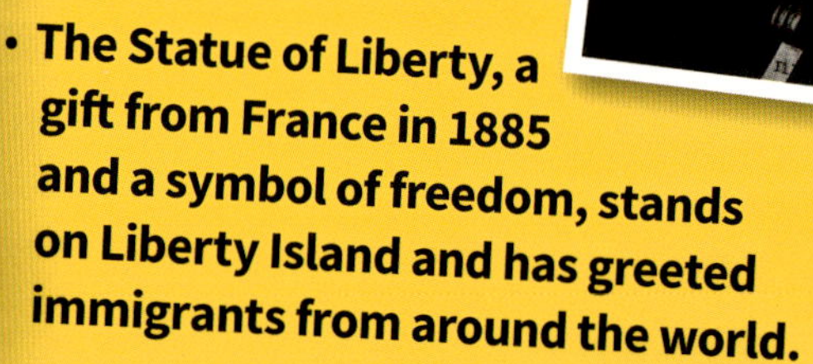

- The Statue of Liberty, a gift from France in 1885 and a symbol of freedom, stands on Liberty Island and has greeted immigrants from around the world.

- Broadway is the theater district of New York City, famous for its plays and musicals.

North Carolina (NC)

★ DID YOU KNOW? ★

- The Venus flytrap, a plant that "eats" insects, is native to Hampstead, North Carolina.

- On December 17, 1903, the Wright brothers completed the first flight of a mechanically propelled airplane over Kitty Hawk, North Carolina.

- Cape Hatteras Lighthouse is the tallest brick lighthouse in the United States.

Nickname: The Tar Heel State

State Capital: Raleigh

Date of Statehood: North Carolina became the 12th state on November 21, 1789

State Bird: Northern Cardinal

State Mammal: Gray Squirrel

State Flower: Dogwood Blossom

FAMOUS PEOPLE FROM NORTH CAROLINA:

★ **Conrad Reed** of Midland, North Carolina, found the first gold to be documented in the United States, in 1799.

★ **Dolley Madison**, born in Guilford County, North Carolina, was married to President James Madison and started the tradition of the annual Easter Egg Roll on the White House lawn.

North Dakota (ND)

Nickname: The Peace Garden State

State Capital: Bismarck

State Bird:
Western Meadowlark

State Mammal:
Nokota Horse

State Flower:
Wild Prairie Rose

FAMOUS PEOPLE FROM NORTH DAKOTA:

★ Before becoming the 26th president of the United States, **Theodore Roosevelt** built a ranch outside of Medora, North Dakota, that he named Elkhorn.

★ **Sacagawea**, a Shoshone woman who was a translator and guide for the Lewis and Clark Expedition, lived in a village in present-day North Dakota.

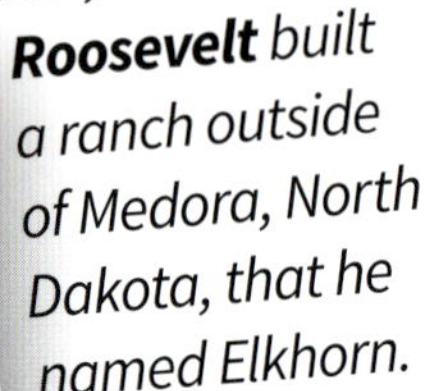

Ohio (OH)

Nickname: The Buckeye State

State Capital: Columbus

Date of Statehood: Ohio became the 17th state on March 1, 1803

State Bird: Northern Cardinal

State Mammal: White-Tailed Deer

State Flower: Red Carnation

- The first hot dog was created in Ohio.

- Ohio's state tree, the Ohio Buckeye, produces a nut that is considered good luck even though it's poisonous.

- Ohio's Goodyear Blimp only weighs between 100 and 200 pounds when it's inflated with helium.

FAMOUS PEOPLE FROM OHIO:

★ **Neil Armstrong**, born in Wapakoneta, Ohio, was the first person to walk on the Moon.

★ **Albert Belmont Graham**, born in Lena, Ohio, founded the 4-H program.

★ **Thomas Edison**, born in Milan, Ohio, had over 1,000 inventions, including the lightbulb.

Oklahoma (OK)

Nickname: The Sooner State

State Capital: Oklahoma City

Date of Statehood: Oklahoma became the 46th state on November 16, 1907

State Bird: Scissor-Tailed Flycatcher

State Mammal: American Bison

State Flower: Oklahoma Rose

FAMOUS PEOPLE FROM OKLAHOMA:

★ *Woody Guthrie*, born in Okemah, Oklahoma, was a singer-songwriter of many ballads, including the famous "This Land Is Your Land."

★ *Wilma Mankiller*, born in Tahlequah, Oklahoma, was the first female chief of the Cherokee Nation.

★ DID YOU KNOW? ★

- The first Girl Scout cookie was sold in Muskogee, Oklahoma, in December 1917.

- Okmulgee, Oklahoma is home to Oklahoma State University, one of the largest technical colleges in the United States.

- Oklahoma has more tornadoes per square mile than any other place in the world.

- Oklahoma City has the only state capitol in the country with a working oil well on its grounds.

- All airplanes in the United States are registered in Oklahoma.

Oregon (OR)

Nickname: The Beaver State

State Capital: Salem

Date of Statehood: Oregon became the 33rd state on February 14, 1859

State Bird: Western Meadowlark

State Mammal: Beaver

State Flower: Oregon Grape

★ DID YOU KNOW? ★

- Crater Lake, with its intensely blue waters, was formed over 6,500 years ago. It is the deepest lake in the United States. 

- The Oregon Trail, which led covered wagons from the East to the West during the 1800s, was 2,000 miles long.

- The "Humungous Fungus" in Grant, Oregon, is the world's biggest organism, covering over 2,300 acres. It's also the oldest, having been around for at least 8,600 years.

- The world's only Bigfoot trap is located in Siskiyou National Forest, in southwestern Oregon.

FAMOUS PEOPLE FROM OREGON:

★ **Beverly Cleary**, *born in McMinnville, Oregon, was an award-winning children's book author.*

★ **Alfred Carlton Gilbert**, *born in Salem, Oregon, invented the Erector Set.*

★ **Linus Pauling**, *born in Portland, Oregon, was awarded the Nobel Prize in Chemistry.*

Pennsylvania (PA)

Nickname: The Keystone State

State Capital: Harrisburg

Date of Statehood: Pennsylvania became the 2nd state on December 12, 1787

State Bird: Ruffed Grouse

State Mammal: White-Tailed Deer

State Flower: Mountain Laurel

★ DID YOU KNOW? ★

- The Philadelphia Zoo was the first zoo in the United States.

- The Liberty Bell in Philadelphia, Pennsylvania, rang in the note of E-flat before it cracked for the last time. No one knows what made it crack.

- Gobbler's Knob is where people gather every February 2, Groundhog Day, to learn from Phil the groundhog if spring is upon us or if we will have to endure six more weeks of winter.

FAMOUS PEOPLE FROM PENNSYLVANIA:

★ **Louisa May Alcott**, born in Germantown, Pennsylvania, wrote Little Women.

★ **Rachel Carson** was a pioneer of environmentalism and author of many books about nature including Silent Spring.

Rhode Island (RI)

FAMOUS PEOPLE FROM RHODE ISLAND:

★ *George M. Cohan, born in Providence, Rhode Island, wrote the song "Yankee Doodle Dandy," among others.*

★ *Gilbert Stuart, born in Saunderstown, Rhode Island, painted the portrait of George Washington that appears on the one dollar bill.*

Nickname: The Ocean State

State Capital: Providence

Date of Statehood: Rhode Island became the 13th state on May 29, 1790

State Bird: Rhode Island Red Rooster

State Flower: Violet

★ DID YOU KNOW? ★

• Rhode Island is the smallest state in the United States. It's 37 miles east to west and 48 miles north to south.

• The first circus in the United States was in Newport, Rhode Island, in 1774.

• Portsmouth, Rhode Island, has the oldest schoolhouse in the United States. It was built in 1716.

South Carolina (SC)

★ **DID YOU KNOW?** ★

- Bishopville, South Carolina, is the home of the Pearl Fryar Topiary Garden, where you can see throwaway plants transformed into amazing sculptures.

- Beaufort, South Carolina, showcases kazoos at its Kazoo Museum and Factory.

Nickname: The Palmetto State

State Capital: Columbia

Date of Statehood: South Carolina became the 8th state on May 23, 1788

State Bird: Carolina Wren

State Mammal: White-Tailed Deer

State Flower: Yellow Jessamine

FAMOUS PEOPLE FROM SOUTH CAROLINA:

★ **Strom Thurmond**, born in Edgefield, South Carolina, was the only United States senator to be elected by a write-in vote. He worked in politics until he was 100 years old.

★ **James Brown**, a musician known as the Godfather of Soul, grew up in Barnwell, South Carolina.

South Dakota (SD)

Nickname: Mount Rushmore State

State Capital: Pierre

Date of Statehood: South Dakota became the 40th state on November 2, 1889

State Bird: Chinese Ring-Necked Pheasant

State Mammal: Coyote

State Flower: Pasque Flower

FAMOUS PEOPLE FROM SOUTH DAKOTA

★ *Tasunke Witco (a.k.a. Crazy Horse)*, a Lakota war leader, was born in South Dakota's Black Hills.

★ *Tatanka Iyotake (a.k.a. Sitting Bull)*, a Lakota leader who fought to keep railroad and mining expansion out of the Black Hills of South Dakota.

★ DID YOU KNOW? ★

• Pierre is the capital of South Dakota and is the only capital that doesn't share any of the letters that make up its name with those that make up its state.

• South Dakota's capital, Pierre, is pronounced "peer."

• The world's largest mountain carving is in Mount Rushmore near Keystone, South Dakota. It features the faces of George Washington, Thomas Jefferson, Theodore Roosevelt, and Abraham Lincoln.

Tennessee (TN)

★ DID YOU KNOW? ★

- The live radio show Grand Ole Opry has been running nonstop since 1925 from Nashville, making it the longest-running live radio program in the world.

- More than 3,800 caves can be explored in Tennessee.

- The second-most-visited house in the country is Elvis Presley's Graceland, in Memphis, Tennessee.

Nickname: The Volunteer State

State Capital: Nashville

Date of Statehood: Tennessee became the 16th state on June 1, 1796

State Bird: Mockingbird

State Mammal: Raccoon

State Flower: Iris

FAMOUS PEOPLE FROM TENNESSEE:

★ *Sequoyah (a.k.a. George Gist)*, born in the Cherokee village of Tuskegee on the Tennessee River, invented the Cherokee alphabet.

★ *Andrew Jackson*, the 7th president of the United States, died outside of Nashville, Tennessee, and has his portrait on the twenty dollar bill.

★ *Steve Fossett*, born in Jackson, Tennessee, was the first person to fly solo both across the Pacific Ocean and around the world in a hot-air balloon.

Texas (TX)

Nickname: The Lone Star State

State Capital: Austin

Date of Statehood: Texas became the 28th state on December 29, 1845

State Bird: Mockingbird

State Mammals: Texas Longhorn, Nine-Banded Armadillo

State Flower: Bluebonnet

FAMOUS PEOPLE FROM TEXAS:

★ **Scott Joplin**, born in Texarkana, was dubbed the King of Ragtime.

★ **Lyndon B. Johnson**, born in Stonewall, Texas, was the 36th president of the United States.

★ **George W. Bush**, 46th governor of Texas and 43rd president of the United States.

★ DID YOU KNOW? ★

• Bracken Cave, just north of San Antonio, Texas, is the summer home of millions of Mexican free-tailed bats, making up the world's largest bat colony.

• The Alamo in San Antonio, Texas, was originally built to be a mission and then was the battleground in Texas's fight for independence from Mexico.

• Oil production in Texas represents over 40 percent of the total U.S. output of crude oil.

Utah (UT)

Nickname: The Beehive State

State Capital: Salt Lake City

Date of Statehood: Utah became the 45th state on January 4, 1896

State Bird: California Gull

State Mammal: Rocky Mountain Elk

State Flower: Sego Lily

FAMOUS PEOPLE FROM UTAH:

★ **Lester Wire**, from Salt Lake City, is considered the inventor of the electric traffic light. He was also a detective on the police force.

★ **Philo T. Farnsworth**, born in Beaver, Utah, invented the TV when he was just 14 years old.

★ DID YOU KNOW? ★

- **Rainbow Bridge in Lake Powell, Utah, is the biggest natural bridge in the world.**

- **The Great Salt Lake in Utah is two to nine times saltier than the ocean.**

- **Arches National Park in Moab, Utah, has more than 2,000 natural stone arches, as well as other interesting rock formations. A rock formation has to have at least a 3-foot-wide opening to be considered an arch.**

Vermont (VT)

Nickname: The Green Mountain State

State Capital: Montpelier

Date of Statehood: Vermont became the 14th state on March 4, 1791

State Bird: Hermit Thrush

State Mammal: Morgan Horse

State Flower: Red Clover

★ DID YOU KNOW? ★

- Vermont produces over three million gallons of maple syrup a year, more than any other state in the country.

- Vermont is a major dairy producer with the highest cow to person ratio in the country.

- Wilson "Snowflake" Bentley photographed over 5,000 snowflakes in Jericho, Vermont, and learned that no two snowflakes are alike.

FAMOUS PEOPLE FROM VERMONT:

★ *Elisha Otis*, born in Halifax, Vermont, invented the modern elevator.

★ *Vermont-born* **Calvin Coolidge** *is the only U.S. president born on the Fourth of July.*

Virginia (VA)

★ **James Madison**, the Father of the Constitution and 4th president of the United States.

★ **Booker T. Washington**, an educator and author who was born in Virginia, founded the Tuskegee Institute, one of the country's first schools for African American men and women.

Nickname: Old Dominion

State Capital: Richmond

Date of Statehood: Virginia became the 10th state on June 25, 1788

State Bird: Northern Cardinal

State Flower: Flowering Dogwood

★ DID YOU KNOW? ★

- The Oyster & Maritime Museum in Chincoteague Island, Virginia, is one of the biggest oyster museums in the world.

- Thomas Jefferson's Monticello estate in Charlottesville, Virginia, is topped with the first dome ever installed on a house in America.

- Wild ponies have grazed on Assateague Island for centuries.

Washington (WA)

- It's against the law in Skamania County, Washington, to harass, trap, or kill Bigfoot, Sasquatch, or any other yet-to-be-discovered species.

- The Hoh Rain Forest in the Olympic Peninsula gets an average of 140 inches of rain a year and is one of the biggest rain forests in the United States.

Nickname: The Evergreen State

State Capital: Olympia

Date of Statehood: Washington became the 42nd state on November 11, 1889

State Bird: American Goldfinch

State Mammal: Orca Whale

State Flower: Coast Rhododendron

FAMOUS PEOPLE FROM WASHINGTON:

★ *Robert Joffrey,* born in Seattle, Washington, was a dancer, choreographer, and cofounder of the Joffrey Ballet.

★ *Bill Gates,* born in Seattle, Washington, founded Microsoft and is one of the richest people in the world.

West Virginia (WV)

Nickname: The Mountain State

State Capital: Charleston

Date of Statehood: West Virginia became the 35th state on June 20, 1863

State Bird: Northern Cardinal

State Mammal: Black Bear

State Flower: Rhododendron

FAMOUS PEOPLE FROM WEST VIRGINIA

★ *Pearl S. Buck*, born in Hillsboro, West Virginia, was a writer who was awarded the Nobel Prize in Literature in 1938.

★ *Chuck Yeager*, born in Myra, West Virginia, was the first pilot to travel faster than sound.

★ DID YOU KNOW? ★

- Moundsville, West Virginia, has one of the country's oldest and biggest Native American burial grounds.

- Mother's Day was first observed in West Virginia.

- West Virginia is almost all forest. Around 75 percent of the state is covered by trees.

- The original Golden Delicious apple tree was discovered near Wellsburg, West Virginia, in 1775.

Wisconsin (WI)

Nickname: The Badger State

State Capital: Madison

Date of Statehood: Wisconsin became the 30th state on May 29, 1848

State Bird: American Robin

State Animal: Badger

State Flower: Wood Violet

★ DID YOU KNOW? ★

- Baraboo, Wisconsin, is the only place in the world with all fifteen species of cranes, including the endangered whooping crane.

- Mount Horeb, Wisconsin, houses the world's largest mustard collection in its National Mustard Museum.

- More than 650 different types of cheese are produced in Wisconsin.

FAMOUS PEOPLE FROM WISCONSIN:

★ Famous magician **Harry Houdini** grew up in Milwaukee, Wisconsin.

★ **Frank Lloyd Wright** was a famous architect and designed Fallingwater, a home built on top of a waterfall.

★ **Charles and John Ringling** founded the Ringling Bros. Circus in Baraboo, Wisconsin.

★ **William Frederick Cody (a.k.a. Buffalo Bill)**, *famous for his Wild West shows, founded the city of Cody, Wyoming.*

★ *Jackson Pollock, born in Cody, Wyoming, was an artist known for his drip-and-splatter paintings.*

★ *Shoshone Chief Washakie befriended settlers passing through Wyoming and worked with the U.S. government to protect his tribe.*

Wyoming (WY)

Nickname: The Equality State

State Capital: Cheyenne

Date of Statehood: Wyoming became the 44th state on July 10, 1890

State Bird: Western Meadowlark

State Mammal: American Bison

State Flower: Indian Paintbrush

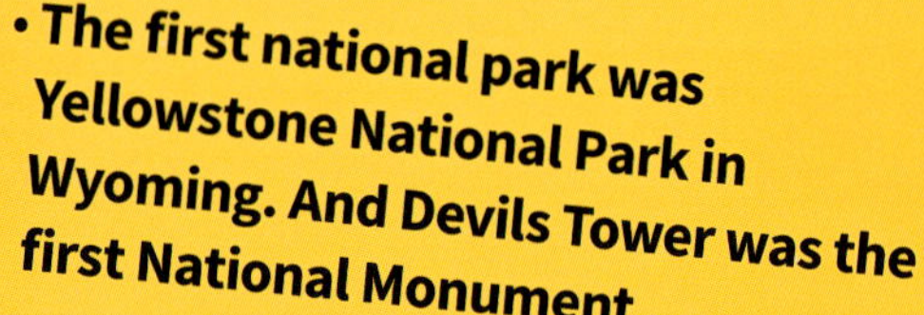

★ DID YOU KNOW? ★

- The first national park was Yellowstone National Park in Wyoming. And Devils Tower was the first National Monument.

- Killpecker Dunes in southern Wyoming are the world's second largest active sand dunes.

- Yellowstone National Park has the most extensive geyser activity in the world. Old Faithful is Yellowstone's most famous geyser and erupts every 60–110 minutes.